Stress Less, Work Better: Managing Work-related Stress Diseases

Katarina Petrova

Copyright © [2023]

Title: Stress Less, Work Better: Managing Work-related Stress Diseases

Author's: Katarina Petrova.

All rights reserved. No part of this publication may be reproduced, stored in a retrieval system, or transmitted in any form or by any means, electronic, mechanical, photocopying, recording, or otherwise, without the prior written permission of the publisher or author, except in the case of brief quotations embodied in critical reviews and certain other non-commercial uses permitted by copyright law.

This book was printed and published by [Publisher's: Katarina Petrova] in [2023]

ISBN:

TABLE OF COJNTENTS

Chapter 1: Understanding Work-related Stress Diseases   06

The Impact of Work-related Stress Diseases on Employees

Recognizing the Signs and Symptoms of Work-related Stress Diseases

Common Work-related Stress Diseases and their Causes

Chapter 2: The Consequences of Work-related Stress Diseases   12

Negative Effects on Physical Health

Impaired Mental Well-being

Strained Interpersonal Relationships and Social Life

Chapter 3: Identifying the Root Causes of Work-related Stress Diseases   18

Excessive Workload and Job Demands

Lack of Control and Autonomy in the Workplace

Poor Work-life Balance and Burnout

Chapter 4: Strategies for Managing and Preventing Work-related Stress Diseases 24

Building Resilience and Coping Mechanisms

Effective Time Management Techniques

Establishing Boundaries and Prioritizing Self-care

Chapter 5: Seeking Support and Resources for Managing Work-related Stress Diseases 30

Utilizing Employee Assistance Programs

Seeking Professional Help from Therapists or Counselors

Connecting with Supportive Colleagues and Building a Network

Chapter 6: Creating a Healthy Work Environment 36

Promoting Work-life Balance Initiatives

Encouraging Open Communication and Feedback Channels

Implementing Stress Management Programs and Policies

Chapter 7: Cultivating a Positive Mindset for Managing Work-related Stress Diseases 42

Practicing Mindfulness and Meditation Techniques

Developing a Growth Mindset and Reshaping Negative Thoughts

Finding Meaning and Purpose in Work

Chapter 8: Sustaining Long-term Well-being and Preventing Work-related Stress Diseases 48

Maintaining Healthy Habits and Lifestyle Choices

Regular Physical Exercise and Relaxation Techniques

Continual Learning and Professional Development

Chapter 9: Overcoming Work-related Stress Diseases and Thriving in the Workplace 55

Setting Realistic Goals and Celebrating Achievements

Embracing Work-life Integration and Flexibility

Fostering a Supportive and Collaborative Work Culture

Chapter 10: Conclusion 61

Recap of Key Strategies for Managing Work-related Stress Diseases

Empowering Employees to Take Control of their Well-being

Inspiring a Stress-less, Productive Work Environment

Chapter 1: Understanding Work-related Stress Diseases

The Impact of Work-related Stress Diseases on Employees

In today's fast-paced and competitive work environment, employees often find themselves dealing with an overwhelming amount of stress. This stress not only affects their productivity and efficiency but also has a detrimental impact on their overall health. In this subchapter, we will delve into the various work-related stress diseases that employees commonly face and explore the profound impact they can have on their lives.

One of the most prevalent stress-caused diseases is anxiety. Constant pressure to meet deadlines, achieve targets, and maintain high performance takes a toll on employees' mental well-being. Anxiety can manifest through symptoms like restlessness, irritability, difficulty concentrating, and even panic attacks. If left unaddressed, anxiety can significantly impair an employee's ability to function effectively, both professionally and personally.

Another common stress-related disease is depression. The incessant demands and the feeling of being overwhelmed by work responsibilities often lead employees to experience a deep sense of sadness and hopelessness. Depression can severely impact an employee's motivation, energy levels, and overall sense of satisfaction, making it challenging to perform at their best.

Physical ailments are also prevalent among employees facing work-related stress. Chronic stress can weaken the immune system, making individuals more susceptible to illnesses such as colds, flu, and other infections. Additionally, prolonged stress can contribute to the development of cardiovascular diseases, high blood pressure, and even digestive problems. These physical ailments not only affect an employee's health but also result in increased absenteeism, decreased productivity, and higher healthcare costs.

Furthermore, work-related stress diseases can have a profound effect on an employee's personal life. The constant pressure and long working hours can strain relationships with family and friends, leading to feelings of isolation and loneliness. Moreover, the inability to switch off from work and relax can lead to a poor work-life balance, negatively impacting the employee's overall quality of life.

Recognizing the impact of work-related stress diseases on employees is crucial for both individuals and organizations. Employees need to proactively address stress, adopt healthy coping mechanisms, and seek support when needed. On the other hand, organizations must implement policies and practices that promote a healthy work environment, encourage work-life balance, and provide resources for managing stress effectively.

In conclusion, work-related stress diseases can have a significant impact on employees' mental and physical well-being, as well as their personal and professional lives. It is imperative for employees to understand the signs and symptoms of stress-related diseases and take proactive steps to manage and mitigate the effects. By prioritizing mental and physical health, employees can lead happier, healthier, and more productive lives.

Recognizing the Signs and Symptoms of Work-related Stress Diseases

In today's fast-paced and demanding work environments, it is crucial for employees to be aware of the signs and symptoms of work-related stress diseases. Stress-caused diseases can have a significant impact on both our physical and mental well-being, affecting our overall productivity and job satisfaction. By recognizing these signs early on, employees can take proactive steps to manage and mitigate the negative effects of work-related stress.

One of the primary indicators of work-related stress diseases is persistent fatigue and exhaustion. Feeling tired even after a full night's sleep, lacking energy throughout the day, and experiencing difficulty in concentrating are all common signs of excessive stress. These symptoms can lead to decreased productivity, errors in work, and a general feeling of being overwhelmed.

Another common manifestation of work-related stress diseases is an increased susceptibility to illnesses. When our bodies are under constant stress, our immune system weakens, making us more vulnerable to infections, colds, and other ailments. Frequent headaches, stomach problems, and a weakened immune system are all red flags that should not be ignored.

Mental health issues are also prevalent among individuals experiencing work-related stress. Feelings of constant anxiety, irritability, and mood swings can all indicate the presence of stress-caused diseases. Additionally, employees may experience difficulty in sleeping, loss of appetite, and an overall sense of dissatisfaction with their work and personal lives.

Recognizing the signs and symptoms of work-related stress diseases is the first step towards addressing these issues. As employees, it is essential to prioritize our well-being and take necessary measures to manage stress effectively. Seeking support from colleagues, supervisors, or professional counselors can provide valuable guidance and assistance in developing coping mechanisms.

Implementing stress management techniques such as regular exercise, meditation, and time management strategies can also alleviate the symptoms of work-related stress diseases. Additionally, setting clear boundaries between work and personal life, and practicing self-care can contribute to a healthier work-life balance.

By recognizing and addressing the signs and symptoms of work-related stress diseases, employees can take control of their well-being and work towards a healthier, more productive work environment. Remember, managing stress is a shared responsibility, and organizations should also promote a culture that prioritizes employee well-being. Together, we can stress less and work better.

Common Work-related Stress Diseases and their Causes

In today's fast-paced and demanding work environments, stress has become an inevitable part of our professional lives. The constant pressure to meet deadlines, handle challenging tasks, and maintain a work-life balance can take a toll on our mental and physical well-being. This subchapter aims to shed light on the most common work-related stress diseases and their causes, providing employees with valuable insights to manage their stress levels effectively.

One of the most prevalent stress-caused diseases is anxiety. Anxiety disorders can manifest in various forms, such as generalized anxiety disorder (GAD), panic disorder, or social anxiety disorder. These conditions are often triggered by excessive workloads, unrealistic expectations, or a hostile work environment. Constant worry, restlessness, and difficulty concentrating are some common symptoms that employees may experience when dealing with anxiety.

Depression is another serious consequence of chronic work-related stress. Prolonged periods of stress can deplete individuals of their energy, motivation, and joy, leading to feelings of sadness, hopelessness, and a loss of interest in activities they once enjoyed. The isolation and lack of support at the workplace can exacerbate these symptoms. Employees must recognize and seek help for depression to prevent its long-term negative impact on their well-being.

Work-related stress can also manifest as physical ailments. One such disease is cardiovascular disorders. The constant pressure and high levels of stress hormones can lead to hypertension, heart disease, and even heart attacks. Employees with sedentary jobs or those who struggle to maintain a healthy work-life balance are particularly at risk.

Another common stress-related disease is musculoskeletal disorders (MSDs). These are often caused by poor ergonomics, repetitive motions, or prolonged sitting. Conditions like chronic back pain, carpal tunnel syndrome, and tendonitis can significantly impact an individual's ability to perform their job effectively. Employers should prioritize creating a supportive work environment with ergonomic furniture and providing regular breaks to prevent the development of MSDs.

In conclusion, work-related stress can lead to a variety of diseases that can have a detrimental impact on employees' physical and mental well-being. Recognizing the signs and causes of these stress-related diseases is crucial for employees to take proactive steps in managing their stress levels. By adopting healthy coping mechanisms, seeking support, and creating a work-life balance, employees can significantly reduce the risk of developing these diseases and lead a healthier and more fulfilling professional life.

Chapter 2: The Consequences of Work-related Stress Diseases

Negative Effects on Physical Health

Stress is a prevalent issue in today's fast-paced and demanding work environments, and its impact on physical health should not be underestimated. Chronic stress can lead to a range of stress-caused diseases that can significantly affect employees' overall well-being. Understanding these negative effects is crucial in order to effectively manage work-related stress and mitigate its impact on physical health.

One of the primary negative effects of chronic stress on physical health is the increased risk of cardiovascular diseases. Prolonged exposure to stress hormones, such as cortisol, can lead to elevated blood pressure, heart rate, and cholesterol levels. This, in turn, raises the risk of heart attacks, strokes, and other cardiovascular problems. Employees who experience chronic stress should be aware of these risks and take proactive steps to reduce stress levels, such as engaging in regular exercise, practicing relaxation techniques, and seeking support from healthcare professionals.

Furthermore, chronic stress can weaken the immune system, making individuals more susceptible to infections and illnesses. When stress hormones are constantly released, the body's ability to fight off viruses and bacteria decreases. This can result in frequent colds, flu, and other infections. Employees should be mindful of the impact of stress on their immune system and take steps to strengthen it, such as getting adequate sleep, eating a balanced diet, and practicing stress-reducing activities like yoga or meditation.

In addition to cardiovascular diseases and weakened immunity, chronic stress can also contribute to digestive problems. Stress can disrupt the normal functioning of the digestive system, leading to issues like stomachaches, acid reflux, and irritable bowel syndrome (IBS). Employees should pay attention to any gastrointestinal symptoms they may experience and seek medical guidance if necessary. Adopting a healthy diet, managing stress through relaxation techniques, and maintaining a regular exercise routine can help alleviate these digestive issues.

It is essential for employees to recognize the negative effects of chronic stress on their physical health and take necessary steps to prevent stress-related diseases. By practicing stress management techniques, seeking support, and maintaining a healthy lifestyle, employees can effectively combat the negative impact of stress on their physical well-being. Prioritizing self-care and stress reduction can ultimately lead to better health outcomes and a happier, more balanced work-life.

Impaired Mental Well-being

In today's fast-paced and demanding work environments, it is not uncommon for employees to experience stress-related diseases. One of the most prevalent and concerning issues faced by workers is impaired mental well-being. This subchapter aims to shed light on the impact of stress on mental health and provide practical strategies to alleviate and manage these challenges.

Stress is a natural response to the demands and pressures we face in our daily lives. However, when stress becomes chronic or overwhelming, it can have severe consequences on our mental well-being. Prolonged exposure to stressful situations in the workplace can lead to anxiety, depression, and other mental health disorders. These conditions not only affect individuals personally but also impact their productivity, job satisfaction, and overall quality of life.

Recognizing the signs of impaired mental well-being is crucial for employees. Common symptoms include persistent feelings of sadness, irritability, difficulty concentrating, changes in appetite or sleep patterns, and a lack of interest in activities once enjoyed. If you are experiencing any of these symptoms, it is essential to seek support and take proactive steps towards improving your mental health.

One effective strategy to manage impaired mental well-being is to develop stress management techniques. Learning to identify and address stress triggers can significantly reduce the impact of stress on your mental health. Engaging in regular exercise, practicing mindfulness and relaxation techniques, and establishing a healthy work-life balance are all effective ways to combat stress.

Additionally, seeking social support is paramount. Talking to trusted colleagues, friends, or family members about your challenges can provide a sense of relief and help you gain perspective. Many organizations also offer employee assistance programs or counseling services, which can be invaluable in managing stress-related mental health issues.

Creating a positive and supportive work environment is crucial for preventing impaired mental well-being among employees. Employers should foster a culture that prioritizes mental health and provides resources and support systems for their workforce. Implementing flexible work arrangements, offering regular breaks, and promoting open communication are just a few ways organizations can contribute to a mentally healthy workplace.

Remember, your mental well-being is as important as your physical health. By recognizing the signs, seeking support, and implementing effective stress management strategies, you can protect yourself from stress-related diseases and create a healthier and more fulfilling work life.

Strained Interpersonal Relationships and Social Life

In the fast-paced and demanding world of work, it is not uncommon for employees to experience strained interpersonal relationships and a diminished social life. The constant pressure to meet deadlines, exceed expectations, and adapt to ever-changing work environments can significantly impact our relationships with colleagues, friends, and family members. This subchapter aims to shed light on the effects of work-related stress on our interpersonal connections and provide practical strategies to improve and restore our social lives.

One of the most noticeable consequences of work-related stress is the strain it puts on our relationships with colleagues and peers. As stress levels rise, so does the likelihood of conflicts, misunderstandings, and breakdowns in communication. The constant pressure to perform can lead to increased irritability, impatience, and a lack of empathy towards others. This not only affects our professional relationships but can also spill over into our personal lives, making it difficult to maintain healthy connections outside of work.

Additionally, work-related stress often consumes a significant amount of our time and energy, leaving us with little motivation or capacity to engage in social activities. Exhaustion and burnout can make it challenging to find the energy to attend social events, spend quality time with loved ones, or partake in hobbies and interests that bring us joy. Consequently, our social lives can suffer, leading to feelings of isolation and loneliness.

To address these challenges, it is crucial for employees to prioritize self-care and find a healthy work-life balance. Setting boundaries and learning to say no when necessary can help manage work-related stress and create more time for social activities. Regularly engaging in stress-reducing techniques such as exercise, meditation, or hobbies can also help restore energy levels and improve overall well-being.

Furthermore, open and honest communication with colleagues and loved ones is vital for maintaining healthy relationships. Sharing our feelings and concerns with trusted individuals can foster understanding and support. Seeking professional help, such as counseling or therapy, can also provide valuable tools for managing stress and improving interpersonal connections.

By recognizing the impact of work-related stress on our interpersonal relationships and social lives, employees can take proactive steps to prioritize their well-being. By implementing strategies to manage stress, setting boundaries, and nurturing relationships, individuals can restore balance and experience a more fulfilling and enriching social life.

Chapter 3: Identifying the Root Causes of Work-related Stress Diseases

Excessive Workload and Job Demands

In today's fast-paced and competitive work environment, employees often face excessive workloads and job demands that can lead to stress-related diseases. This subchapter aims to shed light on the detrimental effects of such work conditions and provide practical strategies to manage and reduce stress in the workplace.

Excessive workload refers to a situation where employees are overwhelmed with an unrealistic amount of tasks, deadlines, and responsibilities. This overwhelming pressure can lead to chronic stress, which has been linked to various health problems, including anxiety, depression, high blood pressure, and heart diseases. Additionally, job demands such as long working hours, constant multitasking, and lack of control over one's work can further exacerbate the negative impact on employees' well-being.

Recognizing the signs of excessive workload and job demands is crucial for employees to take proactive steps in managing their stress levels. Some common indicators include feeling constantly overwhelmed, experiencing physical symptoms like headaches or sleep disturbances, and a decline in job satisfaction and motivation. It is essential for employees to prioritize their well-being and take action to address these issues.

To manage excessive workload and job demands, employees can adopt various strategies. Firstly, effective time management techniques, such as prioritizing tasks, setting realistic deadlines, and delegating responsibilities, can help alleviate work-related stress. Learning to say no and setting boundaries are also vital in preventing the accumulation of excessive workload.

Furthermore, promoting open communication with supervisors and colleagues is crucial. Employees should feel comfortable expressing their concerns about the workload and discussing potential solutions. This can lead to a collaborative effort in finding ways to redistribute tasks or explore more efficient work processes.

Taking regular breaks and engaging in stress-reducing activities during non-work hours is equally important. Engaging in physical exercise, practicing mindfulness techniques, or pursuing hobbies can help employees relax and recharge, reducing the negative impact of work-related stress.

Lastly, seeking professional support is highly recommended. Employers often provide resources like employee assistance programs or counseling services to help employees cope with stress. Additionally, healthcare professionals can offer personalized advice and support tailored to individual needs.

In conclusion, excessive workload and job demands can have severe implications on employees' mental and physical health. By recognizing the signs of excessive workload and implementing effective stress management strategies, employees can mitigate the negative impact and achieve a healthier work-life balance. Prioritizing self-care and seeking support when needed are essential steps in reducing stress-related diseases caused by work-related stress.

Lack of Control and Autonomy in the Workplace

In today's fast-paced and demanding work environment, employees often find themselves grappling with high levels of stress. This stress can lead to various work-related diseases, impacting both physical and mental health. One significant contributor to this growing problem is the lack of control and autonomy in the workplace.

Many employees feel powerless and restricted in their roles, unable to make decisions or have a say in how their work is conducted. This lack of control can be highly detrimental to their overall well-being, leading to increased stress levels and a range of stress-caused diseases.

When employees lack control, they often feel as though they are merely cogs in a machine, with no control over their own destiny. This can lead to feelings of frustration, helplessness, and a general sense of being overwhelmed. The constant pressure to meet deadlines and deliver results without any input or influence can take a toll on both physical and mental health.

Research has shown that individuals who have a higher level of control and autonomy in their work experience lower levels of stress and are generally more satisfied with their jobs. This is because having control over one's work allows for a sense of ownership and accomplishment, leading to increased motivation and productivity.

Organizations need to recognize the importance of providing employees with a certain degree of control and autonomy in their roles. Empowering employees to make decisions, participate in problem-solving, and have a voice in the decision-making process can go a long way in reducing stress levels and preventing stress-caused diseases.

Creating a work culture that values employee autonomy and control can have numerous benefits, including increased job satisfaction, better work-life balance, and improved overall well-being. Employers can achieve this by promoting open communication, fostering a supportive environment, and providing opportunities for skill development and growth.

In conclusion, the lack of control and autonomy in the workplace is a significant contributing factor to the prevalence of stress-caused diseases among employees. Recognizing the importance of empowering employees and providing them with a sense of control over their work can lead to a healthier and more productive workforce. By addressing this issue, employers can create a work environment that promotes employee well-being and ultimately leads to better overall organizational success.

Poor Work-life Balance and Burnout

In today's fast-paced and competitive work environment, finding a balance between work and personal life has become increasingly challenging. Many employees find themselves constantly juggling deadlines, meetings, and responsibilities, leaving little time for relaxation and self-care. This lack of work-life balance can have severe consequences on our mental and physical health, leading to burnout and the onset of stress-caused diseases.

Burnout is a state of chronic physical and emotional exhaustion that is often accompanied by feelings of cynicism and detachment from work. It occurs when the demands of work consistently outweigh the resources available, leaving individuals feeling overwhelmed and drained. This can have a significant impact on our overall well-being, affecting our productivity, relationships, and overall quality of life.

One of the main contributors to poor work-life balance is the blurred boundaries between work and personal life. With the advent of technology, employees are now accessible around the clock, making it difficult to disconnect and recharge. Constantly checking emails and responding to work-related requests outside of working hours can prevent us from fully engaging in our personal lives, leading to increased stress levels and decreased satisfaction.

To combat poor work-life balance and prevent burnout, it is crucial for employees to prioritize self-care and set clear boundaries between work and personal life. This means learning to say no when necessary, delegating tasks, and creating a schedule that allows for regular breaks and time with loved ones. It is also essential to establish a support system, both at work and outside, where employees can seek advice, guidance, and emotional support.

Employers also have a role to play in promoting a healthy work-life balance. They can implement policies that encourage flexible working hours, remote work options, and provide resources for stress management and wellness programs. By recognizing the importance of work-life balance and actively supporting their employees' well-being, employers can create a positive and productive work environment.

In conclusion, poor work-life balance and burnout have become prevalent issues in today's society, leading to stress-caused diseases and diminished quality of life. It is essential for employees to take proactive steps to prioritize self-care and establish clear boundaries between work and personal life. Likewise, employers should foster a supportive work culture that promotes work-life balance and provides resources for stress management. By addressing these issues, we can reduce the risk of burnout and create a healthier and more fulfilling work experience.

Chapter 4: Strategies for Managing and Preventing Work-related Stress Diseases

Building Resilience and Coping Mechanisms

In today's fast-paced and demanding work environments, stress has become an unfortunate companion for many employees. The constant pressure to meet deadlines, fulfill responsibilities, and juggle multiple tasks can take a toll on both physical and mental well-being. Stress often leads to a host of work-related diseases, affecting employees' productivity, engagement, and overall quality of life. However, it is possible to combat these stress-caused diseases by building resilience and adopting effective coping mechanisms.

Resilience is the ability to bounce back from challenging situations and adapt to change. It is a crucial trait for employees to develop in order to navigate the ups and downs of their professional lives successfully. To build resilience, it is important to focus on self-care. This includes prioritizing sleep, exercise, and a healthy diet. Taking breaks throughout the workday and engaging in activities that bring joy and relaxation can also help rejuvenate the mind and body. Additionally, seeking social support from colleagues, friends, or family members can provide a much-needed outlet for stress and anxiety.

Coping mechanisms are strategies individuals employ to manage stress and its associated diseases. There are various coping mechanisms that can be effective in different situations. One such mechanism is mindfulness meditation, which involves being fully present in the moment and observing one's thoughts and emotions without judgment. This practice can help employees manage stress by promoting relaxation and reducing negative thinking patterns.

Another coping mechanism is time management. By prioritizing tasks, setting realistic goals, and breaking down larger projects into smaller, manageable steps, employees can regain a sense of control over their workloads. This approach can alleviate stress and prevent the feeling of being overwhelmed.

Furthermore, effective communication is essential in coping with stress at work. Expressing concerns, seeking feedback, and setting boundaries with coworkers and supervisors can help reduce tension and improve work relationships. Additionally, seeking professional help, such as counseling or therapy, can provide employees with the necessary tools and support to manage stress and related diseases.

In conclusion, building resilience and adopting effective coping mechanisms are crucial for employees to combat stress-caused diseases. By prioritizing self-care, seeking social support, practicing mindfulness, managing time effectively, and fostering open communication, employees can reduce stress levels and improve their overall well-being. Remember, it is essential to take care of oneself in order to work better and live a healthier, more fulfilling life.

Effective Time Management Techniques

In today's fast-paced and demanding work environment, stress-related diseases have become increasingly prevalent among employees. The constant pressure to meet deadlines, juggle multiple tasks, and maintain work-life balance can take a toll on our physical and mental well-being. However, with the right time management techniques, you can effectively reduce stress and improve productivity. This subchapter aims to provide employees with practical strategies to manage their time efficiently and minimize the risk of stress-caused diseases.

One of the most effective time management techniques is prioritization. Start each day by identifying your most important tasks and allocating time for them. This allows you to focus on high-value activities and ensures that crucial deadlines are met. By eliminating unnecessary distractions and staying focused on priority tasks, you can enhance your productivity and reduce stress levels.

Another valuable technique is setting realistic goals and breaking them down into smaller, manageable tasks. This approach helps to prevent overwhelm and allows you to make steady progress towards larger objectives. By breaking tasks into smaller steps, you can maintain a sense of accomplishment and motivation, leading to increased job satisfaction and reduced stress.

Additionally, effective time management involves learning to delegate tasks when necessary. Recognize your limitations and identify tasks that can be assigned to others. Delegation not only frees up your time for more important responsibilities but also promotes teamwork and collaboration within the workplace.

Furthermore, implementing effective communication strategies is crucial for efficient time management. Clear and concise communication ensures that everyone is on the same page, minimizing misunderstandings and avoiding time-consuming rework. Regularly update your colleagues and superiors on your progress, and don't hesitate to ask for assistance or clarification when needed.

Lastly, it is essential to schedule regular breaks throughout the day. Research has shown that taking short breaks improves focus and productivity. Use this time to relax, stretch, or engage in activities that help you recharge. By incorporating regular breaks into your schedule, you can maintain high levels of energy and reduce the risk of burnout.

In conclusion, mastering effective time management techniques is crucial for employees dealing with stress-caused diseases. By prioritizing tasks, setting realistic goals, delegating when necessary, communicating effectively, and scheduling regular breaks, employees can reduce stress levels, improve productivity, and achieve a healthier work-life balance. Implementing these techniques will not only benefit individuals but also contribute to a more positive and productive work environment overall.

Establishing Boundaries and Prioritizing Self-care

In today's fast-paced and demanding work environment, it is easy for employees to become overwhelmed and experience stress-related diseases. However, by establishing clear boundaries and prioritizing self-care, individuals can effectively manage work-related stress and improve their overall well-being.

Setting boundaries is crucial to maintaining a healthy work-life balance and preventing stress-related diseases. It is essential to clearly define your working hours and communicate them to your colleagues and superiors. By doing so, you can protect your personal time and prevent work from encroaching into your personal life. Additionally, establishing boundaries around email and other communication channels can help prevent constant interruptions and allow for uninterrupted focus on important tasks.

Another aspect of establishing boundaries is learning to say no when necessary. Many employees feel pressured to take on additional tasks or work overtime, even when it is not feasible. By setting realistic expectations and understanding your limits, you can avoid overextending yourself and experiencing burnout. Remember, it is okay to prioritize your well-being and decline additional responsibilities when necessary.

Prioritizing self-care is equally important in managing work-related stress and preventing stress-related diseases. Engaging in activities that promote relaxation and rejuvenation can help reduce stress levels and improve overall mental and physical health. This could include practicing mindfulness or meditation, engaging in regular exercise, or pursuing hobbies and interests outside of work. Taking regular breaks throughout the workday and ensuring adequate sleep are also crucial aspects of self-care that should not be overlooked.

Furthermore, it is essential to create a support system both within and outside of the workplace. Building positive relationships with colleagues can provide a sense of belonging and support during challenging times. Additionally, seeking professional help from therapists or counselors can offer valuable guidance and coping strategies for managing stress.

In conclusion, establishing boundaries and prioritizing self-care are fundamental in managing work-related stress and preventing stress-related diseases. By clearly defining boundaries, learning to say no, practicing self-care activities, and seeking support when needed, employees can effectively manage their well-being and work more efficiently. Remember, taking care of yourself is not a luxury but a necessity, and by doing so, you can lead a healthier and more fulfilling professional life.

Chapter 5: Seeking Support and Resources for Managing Work-related Stress Diseases

Utilizing Employee Assistance Programs

In today's fast-paced work environment, stress has become an inevitable part of our daily lives. Long working hours, tight deadlines, and demanding expectations can all contribute to stress-related diseases. However, employers have recognized the importance of addressing these issues and have implemented various programs to support their employees' mental well-being. One such program is the Employee Assistance Program (EAP).

Employee Assistance Programs are designed to provide confidential assistance to employees who may be experiencing work-related stress or personal problems that affect their job performance. These programs offer a wide range of services, including counseling, referral services, and educational resources, all aimed at helping employees manage stress and improve their overall well-being.

One of the key benefits of utilizing an EAP is the access to professional counseling services. Trained professionals can help employees identify and manage stressors, develop coping strategies, and improve their mental health. By offering a safe and confidential space for employees to discuss their concerns, EAPs play a crucial role in reducing stress-related diseases.

Additionally, EAPs often provide referral services to external resources, such as therapists, support groups, or legal advisors, depending on the specific needs of the employee. These resources can further assist individuals in addressing their stress-caused diseases and finding long-term solutions.

Moreover, EAPs offer educational resources to help employees better understand and manage stress. These resources may include workshops, webinars, or self-help materials that provide practical tips and techniques for stress management. By equipping employees with the necessary tools and knowledge, EAPs empower them to take control of their mental well-being and prevent stress-related diseases from escalating.

It's crucial for employees to be aware of their company's Employee Assistance Program and take full advantage of the services offered. By reaching out to an EAP, individuals can proactively address stress-related issues and prevent them from negatively impacting their work and personal lives. Remember, seeking support is a sign of strength, and utilizing an EAP can significantly contribute to a healthier, more balanced life.

In conclusion, Employee Assistance Programs are valuable resources that organizations provide to support their employees' mental well-being. By offering counseling, referral services, and educational resources, EAPs assist individuals in managing stress-caused diseases and improving their overall quality of life. If you are experiencing work-related stress or personal problems that affect your job performance, do not hesitate to reach out to your company's EAP. Remember, taking care of your mental health is essential for achieving a healthier, more productive work-life balance.

Seeking Professional Help from Therapists or Counselors

In our fast-paced and demanding work environments, it is not uncommon for employees to experience stress-related diseases. Whether it's burnout, anxiety, or depression, these conditions can significantly impact our physical and mental well-being, as well as our overall productivity. Recognizing the signs and seeking professional help from therapists or counselors is crucial in managing and overcoming these stress-caused diseases.

Therapists and counselors are trained professionals who specialize in mental health and emotional well-being. They provide a safe and confidential space for individuals to express their thoughts, feelings, and concerns without fear of judgment or reprisal. By seeking their support, employees can gain valuable insights into managing their stress and find effective coping strategies.

One of the benefits of working with therapists or counselors is their ability to help identify the root causes of stress-related diseases. Often, we may not be fully aware of the underlying factors contributing to our stress levels. By delving into our past experiences, thought patterns, and current circumstances, these professionals can help us gain a deeper understanding of ourselves. This self-awareness is essential in making positive changes and breaking free from the cycle of stress.

Moreover, therapists and counselors can teach employees various techniques and tools to manage stress more effectively. These may include relaxation exercises, mindfulness practices, cognitive-behavioral therapy, or stress reduction strategies. By learning and applying these techniques, employees can develop resilience and improve their ability to handle work-related stressors.

Another crucial aspect of seeking professional help is the emotional support provided by therapists and counselors. Dealing with stress-related diseases can feel isolating, and it may be difficult to discuss these issues with family, friends, or colleagues. Therapists and counselors offer a non-judgmental and empathetic ear, providing a safe space to express emotions, fears, and concerns. This emotional support can significantly alleviate the burden of stress, fostering a sense of relief and well-being.

It is important to remember that seeking professional help does not signify weakness or failure. On the contrary, it demonstrates strength and a commitment to self-care. By taking proactive steps to address stress-related diseases, employees can regain control over their lives, improve their work performance, and enhance their overall well-being.

In conclusion, if you find yourself struggling with stress-caused diseases, do not hesitate to seek professional help from therapists or counselors. With their expertise, they can help you identify the root causes, teach effective stress management techniques, and provide the emotional support needed to overcome these challenges. Remember, seeking help is a sign of strength, and it is a crucial step towards a healthier, more fulfilling work life.

Connecting with Supportive Colleagues and Building a Network

In today's fast-paced and demanding work environment, stress-related diseases have become all too common among employees. The negative effects of stress on our physical and mental well-being are well-documented, making it crucial for individuals to actively seek support and build a network of supportive colleagues.

One of the most effective ways to combat stress-caused diseases is by connecting with supportive colleagues. Having a network of like-minded individuals who can empathize with your challenges and provide emotional support can make a world of difference. Supportive colleagues can help you navigate through difficult times, offer guidance, and provide a much-needed sounding board. Their understanding and shared experiences can help alleviate stress and prevent it from escalating into more serious health issues.

Building a network of supportive colleagues starts with being open and approachable. Take the initiative to engage with your coworkers, show genuine interest in their lives, and create opportunities for collaboration and camaraderie. Participating in team-building activities or joining work-related clubs and organizations can be excellent ways to connect with others who share similar interests and concerns.

Additionally, it is important to remember that building a network is a two-way street. Be willing to offer support and lend a helping hand to your colleagues when they need it. By fostering a culture of support and collaboration, you not only benefit from the emotional support of others but also create an environment where everyone can thrive and succeed.

Furthermore, technology can play a significant role in connecting with supportive colleagues. Utilize social media platforms or professional networking sites to connect with coworkers outside the office. Engage in online forums or join groups related to your field of expertise or interests. These virtual communities can provide a valuable support network, even if you work remotely or have limited interaction with colleagues in person.

Ultimately, connecting with supportive colleagues and building a network is an essential aspect of managing work-related stress diseases. By nurturing these relationships, you can find solace in knowing that you are not alone in your struggles and have a support system to lean on. Together, you can navigate the challenges of the workplace, reduce stress, and work towards a happier, healthier professional life.

Chapter 6: Creating a Healthy Work Environment

Promoting Work-life Balance Initiatives

In today's fast-paced and demanding work environment, employees often find it challenging to strike a balance between their personal and professional lives. The consequences of neglecting this balance can be severe, leading to stress-caused diseases that can significantly impact one's overall well-being. Recognizing the importance of work-life balance, many organizations have started prioritizing initiatives to support their employees in achieving a healthier and more fulfilling lifestyle.

Work-life balance initiatives encompass a wide range of strategies and policies aimed at assisting employees in managing their work and personal responsibilities effectively. These initiatives are designed to create a supportive and flexible work environment that fosters employee well-being, engagement, and productivity. By implementing these initiatives, employers acknowledge that a healthy work-life balance is not only beneficial to employees but also crucial for the long-term success of the organization.

One common initiative is the implementation of flexible work arrangements. These arrangements may include telecommuting, flextime, compressed workweeks, or job-sharing options. Such flexibility allows employees to tailor their work schedules to accommodate personal commitments, such as family responsibilities, pursuing hobbies, or attending to personal health needs. By empowering employees to have control over their time, organizations can reduce stress levels and enhance job satisfaction.

Another significant initiative is the promotion of wellness programs. These programs often include activities such as yoga classes, mindfulness workshops, stress management seminars, and access to counseling services. Wellness initiatives aim to enhance employees' physical and mental well-being, providing them with the tools and resources to cope with work-related stress effectively. Encouraging regular exercise, promoting healthy eating habits, and providing access to relaxation spaces are other ways organizations can support their employees in achieving a better work-life balance.

Furthermore, organizations can encourage employees to take advantage of their vacation and paid time off (PTO) benefits. Promoting a culture that values and respects time off allows employees to disconnect from work, recharge, and rejuvenate. This time away from work is essential for reducing stress levels, preventing burnout, and improving overall work performance.

Promoting work-life balance initiatives requires a concerted effort from both employers and employees. Organizations need to foster a supportive culture that prioritizes employee well-being and actively encourages the utilization of these initiatives. Employees, on the other hand, should take responsibility for their own work-life balance by setting boundaries, managing time effectively, and actively participating in the offered programs.

By promoting work-life balance initiatives, organizations can create a healthier and more engaged workforce, reduce the risk of stress-caused diseases, and ultimately improve productivity and employee retention. It is a win-win situation, benefiting both employees and the organization as a whole.

Encouraging Open Communication and Feedback Channels

Subchapter: Encouraging Open Communication and Feedback Channels

In today's fast-paced and demanding work environment, stress has become an unfortunate companion for many employees. The constant pressure to meet deadlines, handle difficult tasks, and navigate office politics can lead to various stress-caused diseases. However, there are ways to combat this epidemic and create a healthier and more productive workplace. One such method is by encouraging open communication and feedback channels.

Open communication is the cornerstone of building a positive work culture. When employees feel comfortable expressing their thoughts, concerns, and ideas, it fosters a sense of belonging and trust within the organization. This, in turn, reduces stress levels and helps prevent stress-caused diseases. By promoting open communication, employers create an environment where employees can freely discuss their work-related challenges and seek support from their colleagues or superiors.

One effective way to encourage open communication is by implementing regular team meetings or feedback sessions. These sessions provide a platform for employees to share their thoughts, offer suggestions, or seek clarification on tasks. Additionally, it allows managers to provide constructive feedback, recognize employee achievements, and address any concerns. This open dialogue helps to mitigate stress as employees feel acknowledged, valued, and supported in their roles.

Another vital aspect of open communication is the establishment of feedback channels. Employees should be encouraged to provide feedback, both positive and constructive, on their work environment, processes, and overall well-being. By actively seeking feedback, employers can gain valuable insights into potential stress triggers within the organization. This information can then be utilized to implement necessary changes, such as workload redistribution, flexible work hours, or stress management programs.

Furthermore, establishing anonymous feedback mechanisms, such as suggestion boxes or online surveys, can empower employees to voice their concerns without fear of retribution. This anonymity promotes honesty and transparency, allowing employers to address issues that may otherwise go unnoticed. Regularly reviewing and acting upon this feedback demonstrates a commitment to employee well-being and fosters a culture of continuous improvement.

Encouraging open communication and feedback channels is a powerful tool in combating stress-caused diseases. By creating an environment where employees feel heard, supported, and empowered, organizations can reduce stress levels and promote overall well-being. This, in turn, leads to higher productivity, improved job satisfaction, and a healthier work-life balance. Remember, communication is key, and together we can make the workplace a stress-free and fulfilling environment.

Implementing Stress Management Programs and Policies

In today's fast-paced and demanding work environment, stress has become a prevalent issue affecting employees across various industries. The negative impact of stress on individuals' physical and mental well-being cannot be overlooked. Stress-caused diseases have become a growing concern, leading to decreased productivity, increased absenteeism, and overall dissatisfaction among employees. To address this pressing issue, organizations must prioritize the implementation of effective stress management programs and policies.

Recognizing the importance of employee well-being, employers have a responsibility to create a supportive and healthy work environment. This subchapter aims to provide employees with valuable insights into the implementation of stress management programs and policies. By understanding the significance of stress management and the available resources, employees can take proactive steps to alleviate and cope with stress-related challenges.

One of the key elements in implementing stress management programs is fostering awareness and education. Employees need to be educated about the causes and symptoms of stress, as well as the potential long-term consequences of stress-caused diseases. By understanding the impact of stress on their health, employees can be motivated to seek support and actively participate in stress management initiatives.

Organizations should also establish clear policies that prioritize employee well-being. This includes promoting work-life balance, encouraging regular breaks, and providing access to resources such as counseling or therapy. Employers should actively create an environment where employees feel comfortable speaking up about their stress levels and seeking assistance without fear of judgment or repercussions.

Furthermore, stress management programs can include a variety of initiatives tailored to meet the diverse needs of employees. These may include stress reduction workshops, mindfulness training, exercise programs, and relaxation techniques. Employers can also explore the possibility of offering flexible work arrangements, such as remote work or flexible hours, to help employees manage their stress more effectively.

By implementing stress management programs and policies, organizations can foster a culture of well-being and support, ultimately leading to healthier and happier employees. Employers and employees must work together to prioritize stress management and create an environment that encourages open communication and proactive support. By addressing stress-related challenges head-on, organizations can enhance productivity, reduce absenteeism, and create a positive work environment that benefits everyone involved.

Chapter 7: Cultivating a Positive Mindset for Managing Work-related Stress Diseases

Practicing Mindfulness and Meditation Techniques

In today's fast-paced and demanding work environment, stress has become a common issue that affects employees' mental and physical health. The constant pressure to meet deadlines, deal with difficult colleagues or clients, and maintain a work-life balance can lead to the development of stress-related diseases. To counter this, it is important for employees to incorporate mindfulness and meditation techniques into their daily routines.

Mindfulness is the practice of being fully present in the moment, without judgment or attachment to thoughts and emotions. By focusing on the present moment, employees can reduce stress, improve concentration, and increase self-awareness. Mindfulness techniques can be easily integrated into daily activities, such as taking short breaks to breathe deeply and observe the surroundings, practicing gratitude, or engaging in mindful eating.

Meditation is a powerful tool that helps employees calm their minds, reduce anxiety, and improve overall well-being. It involves setting aside dedicated time to sit quietly and focus on the breath or a specific object of attention. Regular meditation practice can train the mind to become more resilient and better equipped to handle work-related stressors.

To begin practicing mindfulness and meditation, employees can start with short sessions of just a few minutes a day and gradually increase the duration as they become more comfortable. There are also various apps and online resources available that offer guided meditation sessions, making it easier for employees to incorporate this practice into their busy schedules.

In addition to reducing stress, mindfulness and meditation techniques have been shown to improve creativity, decision-making, and interpersonal relationships. By incorporating these practices into their lives, employees can enhance their overall well-being and work performance.

It is important for organizations to support employees in their journey towards stress management by providing resources and creating a culture that encourages mindfulness and meditation. This can include offering mindfulness workshops, providing access to meditation spaces, or incorporating mindfulness exercises into team meetings.

By practicing mindfulness and meditation techniques, employees can take control of their stress levels, improve their overall health, and create a more positive and productive work environment.

Developing a Growth Mindset and Reshaping Negative Thoughts

In today's fast-paced work environment, employees often face high levels of stress that can lead to various stress-caused diseases. The negative impact of stress on our mental and physical well-being is well-documented, but it's important to remember that we have the power to reshape our thoughts and develop a growth mindset to combat these challenges.

A growth mindset is the belief that our abilities and intelligence can be developed through dedication and hard work. It is the understanding that failure and setbacks are not permanent but rather opportunities for learning and growth. By cultivating a growth mindset, employees can proactively manage work-related stress diseases and improve their overall well-being.

One of the first steps towards developing a growth mindset is becoming aware of our negative thoughts. Negative thoughts often emerge in stressful situations and can hinder our ability to cope effectively. By acknowledging these thoughts, we can start challenging them and replacing them with more positive and constructive ones.

To reshape negative thoughts, it's crucial to practice self-reflection and self-awareness. Take a moment to identify the negative thoughts that frequently arise during stressful situations. Are they rooted in self-doubt or fear of failure? Once you've identified these patterns, actively challenge them by asking yourself if they are based on facts or simply self-limiting beliefs.

Another effective technique for developing a growth mindset is reframing. Reframing involves looking at a situation from a different perspective and finding the positive aspects or opportunities for growth. For example, instead of viewing a demanding project as overwhelming, see it as a chance to develop new skills or showcase your abilities. By reframing our thoughts, we can shift our mindset from one of stress and negativity to one of growth and resilience.

Additionally, fostering a supportive work environment can greatly aid in developing a growth mindset. Encourage open communication, collaboration, and learning opportunities within your workplace. By seeking feedback and embracing challenges, employees can create a culture that values growth and development.

In conclusion, developing a growth mindset and reshaping negative thoughts is essential for managing work-related stress diseases. By recognizing and challenging negative thoughts, reframing situations, and fostering a supportive work environment, employees can proactively combat stress and improve their overall well-being. Embracing a growth mindset allows us to see setbacks as opportunities for growth, leading to increased resilience, productivity, and overall satisfaction in the workplace.

Finding Meaning and Purpose in Work

In today's fast-paced and demanding work environment, it is no surprise that many employees experience high levels of stress. The constant pressure to meet deadlines, exceed targets, and balance personal and professional commitments can take a toll on our mental and physical well-being. This chapter aims to address the issue of stress-caused diseases and provide guidance on how employees can find meaning and purpose in their work to combat these challenges.

An essential aspect of managing work-related stress diseases is finding meaning and purpose in what we do. When we derive a sense of fulfillment and satisfaction from our work, it becomes easier to handle the inevitable stressors that come our way. Finding meaning in work goes beyond merely earning a paycheck; it involves understanding how our contributions make a difference and align with our values and personal goals.

One way to discover meaning in work is by reflecting on our core values and beliefs. Understanding what truly matters to us and how our work aligns with those values can provide a sense of purpose. It is essential to identify the aspects of our job that resonate with our passions, strengths, and goals, and focus on nurturing those areas.

Another effective approach is to seek opportunities for growth and development. Engaging in continuous learning and professional development can not only enhance our skills and knowledge but also provide a sense of progress and accomplishment. By setting clear goals and objectives for ourselves, we can strive for personal and professional growth, thereby finding meaning in our work.

Additionally, building positive relationships at work can significantly impact our sense of purpose. Collaborating with colleagues, supporting one another, and fostering a positive work environment can create a sense of belonging and community. When we feel connected to our colleagues and work as a team, the challenges we face become more manageable, and our work becomes more fulfilling.

Lastly, it is crucial to maintain a healthy work-life balance to find meaning and purpose in our work. When we prioritize our well-being, spend time with loved ones, pursue hobbies, and engage in activities that bring us joy outside of work, we can bring a renewed sense of purpose and energy to our professional lives.

In conclusion, stress-caused diseases are a prevalent concern for many employees in today's work environment. However, by finding meaning and purpose in our work, we can better manage these challenges. By reflecting on our core values, seeking growth opportunities, building positive relationships, and maintaining a healthy work-life balance, we can cultivate a sense of fulfillment and satisfaction in our professional lives.

Chapter 8: Sustaining Long-term Well-being and Preventing Work-related Stress Diseases

Maintaining Healthy Habits and Lifestyle Choices

In today's fast-paced and demanding work environment, stress has become a common factor that affects employees' overall well-being. Prolonged exposure to stress can lead to a range of stress-related diseases, impacting both physical and mental health. However, by adopting healthy habits and making positive lifestyle choices, employees can effectively manage and reduce the impact of stress on their lives.

One of the most crucial aspects of maintaining a healthy lifestyle is prioritizing self-care. This includes getting enough sleep, eating a balanced diet, and engaging in regular physical activity. Sleep is essential for the body to rejuvenate and repair itself, so aim for seven to eight hours of quality sleep each night. Proper nutrition provides the necessary nutrients to support the body's functions and reduce the risk of diseases caused by stress. Incorporate fruits, vegetables, whole grains, and lean proteins into your diet. Additionally, exercise has proven to be a powerful stress-reducer, releasing endorphins and boosting mood. Find an activity you enjoy, whether it's jogging, swimming, or dancing, and make it a regular part of your routine.

In addition to physical health, mental well-being is equally important. Engaging in activities that help manage stress and promote relaxation can be beneficial. Consider practicing mindfulness techniques such as meditation or deep breathing exercises. These techniques can help calm the mind and reduce anxiety. Additionally, finding hobbies or activities that bring joy and fulfillment can provide a much-needed break from work-related stress.

Creating a work-life balance is vital to maintaining a healthy lifestyle. Set clear boundaries between work and personal life, ensuring time for leisure, family, and social activities. Disconnect from work-related devices during non-working hours to allow for relaxation and rejuvenation. Establishing a support system, both at work and in personal life, can provide encouragement and assistance during challenging times.

Lastly, it is crucial to recognize the signs of stress-related diseases and seek professional help when necessary. Regular check-ups with healthcare professionals can help identify any potential health issues and provide guidance on managing stress-related diseases.

By incorporating these healthy habits and lifestyle choices into your daily routine, you can effectively manage work-related stress and reduce the risk of stress-related diseases. Remember, your health and well-being are essential assets that deserve priority attention.

Regular Physical Exercise and Relaxation Techniques

Regular physical exercise and relaxation techniques are essential tools for managing and reducing work-related stress and preventing stress-caused diseases. In today's fast-paced and demanding work environment, many employees find themselves overwhelmed and unable to cope with the mounting pressure. However, incorporating these practices into your daily routine can significantly improve both your physical and mental well-being.

Physical exercise, such as walking, jogging, or participating in sports, is known to release endorphins, the body's natural feel-good hormones. These endorphins not only boost your mood but also help in reducing stress levels. Regular exercise also improves cardiovascular health, increases stamina, and strengthens the immune system, making you more resilient to stress-related diseases.

In addition to physical exercise, relaxation techniques play a crucial role in managing work-related stress. Techniques such as deep breathing exercises, progressive muscle relaxation, and meditation help calm the mind and promote relaxation. These techniques enable you to achieve a state of mental clarity and reduce anxiety, allowing you to tackle work-related challenges more effectively.

Moreover, regular physical exercise and relaxation techniques have been proven to enhance cognitive function, memory, and concentration. By incorporating these practices into your routine, you can improve your overall productivity and work performance. Taking short breaks during work hours to stretch or practice deep breathing exercises can help you recharge and combat the negative effects of stress.

It is important to remember that incorporating physical exercise and relaxation techniques into your routine should not be seen as an additional chore but rather as an investment in your well-being. Start small and gradually increase the duration and intensity of your workouts. Find activities that you enjoy and that fit into your schedule, making it easier to stick with them in the long run.

By making regular physical exercise and relaxation techniques a priority in your life, you will not only reduce the risk of stress-related diseases but also improve your overall quality of life. Take the time to invest in yourself and prioritize self-care. Your body and mind will thank you, and you will be better equipped to handle the challenges that work throws your way.

Continual Learning and Professional Development

In today's fast-paced work environment, employees are constantly faced with new challenges and increased pressure to perform at their best. This can often lead to stress-caused diseases, such as anxiety, depression, and burnout. However, by prioritizing continual learning and professional development, employees can not only mitigate the negative effects of stress but also enhance their overall well-being and work performance.

Continual learning refers to the ongoing process of acquiring new knowledge, skills, and competencies throughout one's career. It is crucial for employees to recognize that learning is not confined to the classroom or formal training sessions. Instead, it can occur through various channels, including on-the-job experiences, mentoring relationships, and self-directed learning.

Professional development, on the other hand, focuses on enhancing specific job-related skills and competencies. This can involve attending workshops, conferences, or seminars, or pursuing additional certifications or advanced degrees. By continuously improving their professional skills, employees can stay up-to-date with industry trends and advancements, making them more valuable assets to their organizations.

Engaging in continual learning and professional development offers several benefits for employees dealing with stress-caused diseases. Firstly, it provides a sense of purpose and motivation, as individuals feel empowered and energized by the acquisition of new knowledge and skills. This renewed enthusiasm can counterbalance the negative effects of stress and help employees develop a more positive mindset.

Secondly, continual learning and professional development enable employees to expand their skill set, making them more adaptable in the face of changing work demands. By broadening their knowledge base, employees can approach tasks and challenges with increased confidence and competence, reducing the likelihood of stress-induced errors or setbacks.

Furthermore, continual learning and professional development contribute to personal growth and career advancement. By actively seeking opportunities to learn and develop, employees demonstrate a commitment to their professional growth and demonstrate their potential for future promotions or career transitions. This increased sense of control over one's career can alleviate stress and enhance overall job satisfaction.

To foster a culture of continual learning and professional development, organizations can provide resources and support to employees, such as access to online training platforms, mentorship programs, or tuition reimbursement for further education. Additionally, managers can encourage employees to set learning goals and provide regular feedback and recognition for their efforts.

In conclusion, continual learning and professional development are vital tools for employees dealing with stress-caused diseases. By embracing a mindset of lifelong learning and actively seeking opportunities to enhance their skills and knowledge, employees can not only alleviate stress but also thrive in their careers. Investing in self-improvement is a proactive approach to managing work-related stress diseases and ultimately leads to increased job satisfaction and overall well-being.

Chapter 9: Overcoming Work-related Stress Diseases and Thriving in the Workplace

Setting Realistic Goals and Celebrating Achievements

In the fast-paced and demanding world of work, stress has become an inevitable part of our lives. The constant pressure to meet deadlines, achieve targets, and excel in our careers can take a toll on our mental and physical well-being. As employees, it is crucial to understand the importance of setting realistic goals and celebrating our achievements to effectively manage stress and prevent stress-caused diseases.

Setting realistic goals is the foundation of a healthy and balanced work life. It involves assessing our capabilities, resources, and limitations to create achievable objectives. By setting realistic goals, we can alleviate the overwhelming pressure that often accompanies unrealistic expectations. It allows us to focus on what truly matters, prioritize our tasks, and work towards our objectives in a more manageable and sustainable manner.

Moreover, celebrating achievements is equally vital in the pursuit of stress management. Taking the time to acknowledge and celebrate our accomplishments not only boosts our self-esteem but also serves as a motivation to continue striving for success. By celebrating achievements, we create a positive work environment that fosters a sense of fulfillment and satisfaction, reducing the risk of stress-caused diseases.

To effectively set realistic goals, it is essential to first identify our strengths and weaknesses. Understanding our capabilities enables us to align our goals with what we can realistically achieve, taking into account the resources and skills available to us. Setting clear and specific goals, accompanied by measurable milestones, provides a roadmap for success and helps us stay focused and motivated. Regularly reassessing and adjusting our goals as necessary is important to ensure that they remain attainable and relevant in the face of changing circumstances.

Celebrating achievements, both big and small, is equally important. It is crucial to acknowledge our accomplishments and the efforts we have put in to reach them. This can be done through various means, such as personal rewards, team recognition, or even a simple acknowledgment from our superiors. By celebrating achievements, we cultivate a culture of appreciation and positivity, fostering a healthier and more productive work environment.

In conclusion, as employees dealing with the challenges of work-related stress, it is crucial to set realistic goals and celebrate our achievements. By doing so, we can effectively manage stress and prevent stress-caused diseases. Setting realistic goals allows us to work towards achievable objectives, minimizing pressure and maximizing productivity. Celebrating achievements boosts our motivation, self-esteem, and overall well-being, creating a positive work environment. By incorporating these practices into our daily lives, we can strive for a healthier and more fulfilling work experience.

Embracing Work-life Integration and Flexibility

In today's fast-paced and demanding work environment, it is crucial for employees to find a balance between their professional and personal lives. The concept of work-life integration and flexibility has gained significant attention as a means to reduce stress-caused diseases and improve overall well-being. This subchapter explores the importance of embracing work-life integration and flexibility and provides practical strategies for employees to achieve a healthier work-life balance.

Work-life integration is a mindset that encourages employees to blend their work and personal lives harmoniously. It acknowledges that work is an essential part of life but should not dominate or overshadow other important aspects such as family, hobbies, and self-care. By embracing work-life integration, employees can experience a sense of fulfillment, happiness, and reduced stress.

Flexibility is a key component of work-life integration. It allows employees to have control over their schedules, enabling them to prioritize personal commitments while still meeting their professional obligations. Flexible work arrangements, such as remote work, flexible hours, and compressed workweeks, can greatly contribute to work-life integration.

To embrace work-life integration and flexibility, employees must first assess their priorities and set boundaries. Understanding what truly matters outside of work helps in creating a clear delineation between personal and professional life. Communicating these boundaries to supervisors and colleagues is essential to ensure they are respected and supported.

Additionally, employees can practice time management techniques to optimize their productivity during work hours. Prioritizing tasks, delegating when necessary, and eliminating distractions can help in achieving a better work-life balance. Taking regular breaks, both short and long, is also crucial for maintaining focus and preventing burnout.

Furthermore, technology can play a vital role in work-life integration. Utilizing productivity apps, project management tools, and communication platforms can streamline work processes, allowing employees to accomplish tasks efficiently and have more time for personal activities.

In conclusion, embracing work-life integration and flexibility is crucial for employees to manage stress-caused diseases and enhance their overall well-being. By prioritizing personal commitments, setting boundaries, practicing effective time management, and utilizing technology, employees can achieve a healthier work-life balance. Employers and organizations that promote and support work-life integration and flexibility are likely to have happier, more productive employees who are less prone to stress-related illnesses.

Fostering a Supportive and Collaborative Work Culture

In today's fast-paced and demanding work environments, stress-related diseases have become increasingly prevalent among employees. The detrimental effects of stress on physical and mental health are well-documented, making it crucial for organizations to prioritize the creation of a supportive and collaborative work culture. By doing so, employers can significantly reduce the risk of stress-related diseases and promote overall well-being among their workforce.

A supportive work culture begins with open communication and mutual respect. Employees should feel comfortable expressing their concerns, ideas, and opinions without fear of judgment or retribution. Encouraging an open-door policy where managers are approachable and receptive to feedback can foster a sense of belonging and trust. This type of environment allows employees to voice their stressors and seek support, which can help alleviate the negative effects of stress.

Collaboration is another key component of a supportive work culture. Encouraging teamwork and providing opportunities for employees to work together on projects can enhance problem-solving abilities and reduce stress. When employees feel supported by their colleagues and have a sense of shared responsibility, the workload becomes more manageable and less overwhelming.

To promote collaboration, organizations should consider implementing regular team-building activities and workshops. These activities can help foster positive relationships, improve communication, and enhance overall teamwork. Additionally, organizations can provide platforms for employees to share their expertise and ideas through cross-departmental collaborations or knowledge-sharing sessions. By embracing teamwork and collaboration, employers can create an environment that promotes a sense of community and support, ultimately reducing stress levels and the risk of stress-related diseases.

Furthermore, organizations should prioritize work-life balance initiatives. Encouraging employees to take regular breaks, providing flexible working hours, and promoting wellness programs can significantly reduce stress levels. Employers can also implement initiatives such as mindfulness or meditation sessions, which have been proven to enhance well-being and reduce stress.

In conclusion, fostering a supportive and collaborative work culture is vital to combat stress-related diseases. By creating an environment that values open communication, collaboration, and work-life balance, organizations can significantly reduce stress levels among employees. Prioritizing employee well-being not only benefits individual employees but also leads to increased productivity and overall success for the organization. It is essential for employers to recognize the importance of nurturing a supportive work culture and take proactive steps towards minimizing stress and promoting a healthier and happier workforce.

Chapter 10: Conclusion

Recap of Key Strategies for Managing Work-related Stress Diseases

In today's fast-paced and competitive work environment, stress has become a common concern for many employees. Prolonged exposure to stress can lead to a range of work-related diseases, which can have a detrimental impact on both physical and mental health. However, there are several effective strategies that employees can adopt to manage and reduce work-related stress diseases, ensuring a healthier and more productive work life.

One of the fundamental strategies is the practice of self-care. By prioritizing self-care activities, such as regular exercise, healthy eating, and sufficient sleep, employees can enhance their overall well-being and resilience to stress. Engaging in physical activities not only helps to release tension but also promotes the production of endorphins, which are natural mood boosters. Eating a balanced diet with nutritious foods can provide the necessary energy and nutrients to combat stress. Additionally, getting enough quality sleep rejuvenates the body and mind, allowing employees to better cope with work-related challenges.

Another vital strategy is effective time management. Employees should learn to prioritize tasks and allocate time appropriately. By setting realistic goals and breaking them down into smaller, manageable steps, individuals can reduce feelings of overwhelm and enhance their productivity. Additionally, it is crucial to establish boundaries and learn to say no when necessary. Overcommitting and taking on excessive workloads can lead to burnout and exacerbate stress-related diseases.

Developing strong support systems is also essential for managing work-related stress diseases. Seeking social support from colleagues, friends, or family members can provide a valuable outlet for expressing emotions and receiving guidance. Engaging in open and honest communication with supervisors or managers about workload concerns or stress-related issues can also lead to collaborative solutions and improved work environments.

Furthermore, implementing stress-reducing techniques, such as mindfulness and relaxation exercises, can significantly alleviate work-related stress diseases. Mindfulness involves focusing on the present moment and cultivating a non-judgmental awareness of thoughts and feelings. This practice can help individuals manage stress by redirecting their attention away from negative thoughts. Relaxation techniques, such as deep breathing exercises, progressive muscle relaxation, or meditation, can help to calm the mind and body, reducing stress levels.

In conclusion, managing work-related stress diseases is crucial for maintaining a healthy work-life balance. By practicing self-care, effective time management, building support systems, and implementing stress-reducing techniques, employees can mitigate the impact of stress on their well-being. By incorporating these strategies into their daily lives, individuals can achieve greater resilience, improved productivity, and ultimately, a more fulfilling work experience.

Empowering Employees to Take Control of their Well-being

In today's fast-paced and demanding work environment, stress has become a common factor affecting employees' well-being. Stress-caused diseases have become a significant concern, leading to decreased productivity, increased absenteeism, and even long-term health issues. However, there are ways for employees to take control of their well-being and effectively manage work-related stress. This subchapter aims to provide valuable insights and practical strategies to empower employees in combating stress-caused diseases.

First and foremost, it is crucial for employees to recognize the signs and symptoms of stress. Stress can manifest in various ways, such as fatigue, irritability, difficulty concentrating, and physical ailments like headaches or stomachaches. By being aware of these indicators, employees can take timely action to address the underlying causes and prevent further escalation.

One effective strategy for managing work-related stress is to establish a work-life balance. Often, employees find it challenging to separate their personal and professional lives, leading to chronic stress. By setting clear boundaries and allocating time for activities outside of work, such as hobbies, exercise, or spending quality time with loved ones, employees can recharge and rejuvenate, reducing the negative impact of stress.

Additionally, adopting healthy lifestyle habits significantly contributes to overall well-being. Regular exercise, a balanced diet, and sufficient sleep are essential components of a healthy lifestyle. Engaging in physical activities not only improves physical health but also helps in reducing stress and boosting mental well-being. Employees should prioritize self-care and allocate time for activities that bring joy and relaxation.

Furthermore, it is crucial for employees to effectively communicate their needs and concerns to their supervisors and colleagues. Open and honest communication fosters a supportive work environment, where employees feel comfortable discussing their stressors and seeking assistance when needed. Employers can also play a significant role by implementing stress management programs, providing resources, and encouraging a positive work culture.

Lastly, employees should be proactive in seeking professional help when required. Mental health professionals, such as therapists or counselors, can provide valuable guidance and support in coping with stress-caused diseases. Seeking help is not a sign of weakness but rather a proactive step towards maintaining overall well-being.

In conclusion, employees must take control of their well-being to effectively manage work-related stress and prevent stress-caused diseases. By recognizing the signs of stress, establishing a work-life balance, adopting healthy lifestyle habits, communicating effectively, and seeking professional help when needed, employees can empower themselves to lead healthier and more fulfilling lives. Remember, your well-being is in your hands, and by taking proactive steps, you can stress less and work better.

Inspiring a Stress-less, Productive Work Environment

In today's fast-paced and demanding work environment, it is common for employees to experience high levels of stress. This constant pressure can often lead to a range of stress-related diseases that can have a significant impact on our physical and mental well-being. However, by taking proactive steps to create a stress-less and productive work environment, we can minimize the risk of developing these health issues and enhance our overall work experience.

One of the key factors in achieving a stress-less work environment is fostering open communication and a supportive culture. Encouraging employees to share their thoughts, concerns, and ideas without fear of judgment or reprisal can create a sense of belonging and unity. By promoting teamwork and collaboration, we can reduce feelings of isolation and create a positive work atmosphere where everyone feels valued and supported.

Furthermore, it is essential to establish clear expectations and realistic goals. Uncertainty and ambiguity can contribute significantly to stress levels. By providing employees with a well-defined job description, clear objectives, and regular feedback, we can help alleviate anxiety and boost productivity. Regular check-ins and performance evaluations can also provide an opportunity to address any concerns or challenges before they escalate.

To create a stress-less work environment, it is crucial to prioritize work-life balance. Encouraging employees to take regular breaks, use their allotted vacation time, and maintain healthy boundaries between work and personal life can prevent burnout and enhance overall well-being. Promoting physical activity and offering wellness programs can also contribute to reducing stress levels and improving overall health.

Additionally, providing employees with the necessary resources and support to manage their workload efficiently is essential. Offering training programs, workshops, and resources to enhance time management, organizational skills, and stress management techniques can empower employees to take control of their work and reduce stress levels.

Finally, it is crucial to lead by example. Managers and leaders should demonstrate a healthy work-life balance, practice effective stress management techniques, and prioritize employee well-being. By modeling these behaviors, they set the tone for a stress-less work environment and inspire others to follow suit.

In conclusion, by creating a stress-less and productive work environment, we can significantly reduce the risk of stress-related diseases and enhance our overall work experience. By fostering open communication, setting clear expectations, prioritizing work-life balance, providing necessary support, and leading by example, we can inspire a healthier and more productive workplace. Remember, your well-being matters, and by taking proactive steps towards stress management, we can work better and live a more fulfilling life.

www.ingramcontent.com/pod-product-compliance
Lightning Source LLC
LaVergne TN
LVHW012047070526
838201LV00082B/3824